It's Your Movie!

It's Your Movie!

Creating the Life You Want

PETER SCHROEDER

Intentional World Publishing

A PGS, Inc. book
Intentional World Publishing
Sedona, AZ 86336

Illustrations © 2005 by Peter and James Schroeder
Book design by Anugito, Artline Graphics
Cover design copyright © 2005 by Peggy Sands
Editing, publicity, and marketing by Thunder Mountain Productions
ISBN 0-9971503-0-5
Library of Congress 2005907343

CONTENTS

Preface

Not that long ago, I met Peter and heard his songs. They were upbeat, melodic, sincere, and refreshing.

An idea popped up before him one day, like a robin in the Spring or a dream you remember, to write an inspirational book using his insights as a group leader and a seminar facilitator, along with his original music and lyrics.

Peter began to write and create and edit and conceive with intention. And it happened!

It's Your Movie! has been born, launched in Sedona, Arizona, where creativity is in the air.

For new as well as experienced readers of books of growth, this concept hits the mark. It's alive with gusto, and a clear focus of … intention. Yes, with intention. This is the way to go!

Be responsible! Be clear and fearless! Go for your higher good! Why not – it's your life, your movie!

This book helps you drop the old conditioning, and gives you new directions. It helps you get ready to live with fresh awareness, to go forward into your full potential.

Come sing with Peter. Give it a try with the sample CD attached to the back cover.

Get ready for a fabulous time … we all love the movies!

Use these ideas in your life today. A brighter future for you, or your misery back. Guaranteed!

Go for it!

Liberty Lincoln, Sedona, AZ

Preview

Every life lived is a script written. Every day, every decision, every moment is part of a developing plot.

Each plot involves twists and surprises, as well as obvious, logical steps as it unfolds. There is the intertwining of numerous subplots, with characters stranger than fiction. And the action builds as personalities become more established in their roles.

In film production, the studio or independent filmmaker chooses the writer, director and actors. They select the location where the film is to be shot. They gather the crew to assist in the production, and deal with the financing. They are in complete control.

In life, who is in control? Does anyone have autonomy? Who picks the locations, writes the script, and chooses the co-stars? Who is taught these things? On the contrary, the standard instructions say to listen to others, who supposedly know better. And so, you listen and follow.

What do you truly control? That's the basic question here. And the answer used in this production is: much more than you realize.

There is always a starting set of circumstances: a location, a cast of characters, and a plot set-up where you enter into an existing story, to grow from a totally dependent child to a mostly independent adult.

Another way of looking at it is evolving from immature to responsible. Wouldn't a responsible adult be in charge of the plot, the scenery, the cast, the crew, the budget, the action, the soundtrack, the script ... the movie? (In this book, the soundtrack is represented at the end of each section as lyrics from songs that actually served as bases for some of the chapters.)

But what happens so often? Others grab the pen that writes your script. They take over your director's chair, where you rightfully belong. You have even let others star in your own production!

And, up until now, the story could be a tragedy. The good guy isn't good enough. The plot remains unresolved, and there is no happy ending.

But plots thicken! Storylines twist in unexpected ways. New supporting characters present themselves, and the hero or heroine emerges at last and overcomes the obstacles to live happily ever after.

Exciting choices, indeed! Choices you can make whenever you choose. At any time, you can reclaim the director's chair, and take back the pen. You can start writing the script, recasting the film, selecting different locations for new scenes that are of your choosing. And shout to the world, "*It's my movie!*"

Because, in reality, you *are* in control. You've always been in control. It's just that you've let some things control you. Things like fear, and shame, and guilt.

Are you ready to start work on the next scene? Why not write it to go through the fear, to drop the shame, and to forgive the guilt? Haven't you carried them long enough?

This is your invitation to sit in that director's chair, and pick up that pen. Start writing. Start directing. *It's Your Movie!*

Introducing the Plot

Suppose that you are the hero or heroine of a movie. And suppose that that movie is your life. Perhaps the plot moves something like this:

You are gazing out at your world, contemplating the dilemma in which you find yourself. Everywhere you turn, you find locked doors and dead-end streets – reasons to feel ·mired in frustration.

You see that much of your world has been set up by others, by society, by institutions. Yet, you admit that some of the obstacles and traps are your own doing. It seems hopeless.

Then, antagonists enter. The conflict is established. You realize who is the enemy, and learn the enemy has many faces. The enemy shows up as the beliefs of your family, friends, and teachers. It shows up as messages you pick up from TV and movies. And the enemy shows up as your own ego – the ego that judges and tries to keep you separate.

The conflict builds because deep inside, you hear a voice that whispers from time to time. That quiet Inner Voice seems to be contradicting what others and the ego are telling you. It is disturbing as it whispers more and more loudly: Open your heart! Let your Light shine!

Eventually, it is what prompts you to become the hero or heroine that you are. For you pay attention to that voice. You heed it because you can ignore it no longer. It persists. You act.

Your strength grows as you listen, and your destiny emerges. The voice transforms into a vibration that you learn to trust.

Your perception shifts. In small ways at first, making a few slight changes in your life. You view things differently, almost with a freshness. You respond in new ways. You act with precise intentions, and react after thoughtful consideration.

But the opposition forces grow, too. These seducers can look so good, talk so sweetly, and seem so justified. So, as the plot turns, it can veer toward defeat or victory. And you know you have the power to contribute to either.

You understand all these things, and you make your choices. You see how change is constant. You accept your power.

Now, all these elements converge to give you hope and resolve. You appreciate your place in the world – your role. And so you use your influence as you feel you should.

Thus, the climax is certain – not in the overcoming of your enemies, or the conclusion of your conflict, but in the liberation of your joy, the expression of your truth, and the love you have for your impact on the whole.

This is cause to celebrate! This is the freedom you have sought all along. Not the end of the movie, but the start of the sequel. Though not before the closing shots, as the credits roll over the setting sun. (Or could it be the rising sun?)

The closing shots are the lessons learned. The knowledge gained forms the new filter through which life is viewed.

As the last shot fades, you are equipped to be a great role model for others, but more importantly, to have your own convictions, and to live with intentions consistent with those convictions.

You hold the pen that writes your script. You direct the cameras that shoot each scene. You choose the location. You cast the future.

All with intention.

1

Opening Scenes

Building The Set
Setting The Stage
The Curtain Rises
Go For The Love

Building the Set

One of the very first considerations when making a film is designing the set – the locations, the scenery, the entrances and exits used by the characters. How has your set been designed and built? Take a closer look: Are there trapdoors and snares, ready to catch those who aren't careful?

Life is full of pitfalls and obstacles that pop up in the most indirect ways. You may think you are doing one thing, when in reality, you are doing something completely different. You think you're giving a gift to someone, but when they don't express gratitude, you're hurt. So, is it a gift, or a deal? I give you something, but there is a condition – you must give me something (gratitude) in return.

And then, there is blame. It's one of the most widely used traps in existence. It's so easy to get caught in the blame trap, because when things don't go the way you want, *someone must be at fault.*

I'm talking about blame with irrefutable justification. No-doubt-about-it, they-deserve-it, and they-are-not-going-to-get-away-with-it *blame!* Is the blame trap part of your set?

Jill used to work for someone she considered arrogant and powerful. She felt he didn't listen to good ideas, and he thought of himself as superior to most. She blamed him for causing her to feel unimportant. And she had many mental conversations with him, where she would argue her point, and get angry. And she blamed him for her anger.

For years this went on in her head. She held a deep resentment and it was redirected to those closest to her. She was trapped by her refusal to let it go. Actually, she never considered that letting go was an option until she heard of the benefit of letting go. She learned that she was the one in pain.

So, she decided to shift her focus by going through a process of forgiveness. Jill substantially reconstructed her set. She began to understand his reasons for being the way he was – his fatherless childhood, and his responsibility for raising a younger brother and sister. She shifted from blame to compassion. She found other ways she could respond to his behavior, such as with curiosity and acceptance.

And she found areas in her life, such as her children and her home, her clients, and her charity work, that made her feel very important, and she realized that his not listening did not mean she was unimportant.

Sound familiar? Hey, from time to time, things get a little challenging. Life happens. And there is little or nothing else to do (that you can think of, in your frenzied state), so you find someone or something else to blame.

And, of course, you then step into the blame trap. Oh, yeah. It's a beauty. One that can hold you for a really long time. You can even share your blame trap with others, who then join you as captives, gladly.

Here's the trap: Whoever blames, suffers. Like Jill.

So what, you say, the blame stays! It's their fault you lost that money, or you got fired, or your nerves are shot, or you have high blood pressure. It's their fault and you can never forgive them! *There is no way!*

Yes, there is a way. You can forgive.

You can come to a point in your life when you realize you really haven't been "punishing" the perpetrator(s) by blaming and holding on to the blame, you've just been tormenting yourself. And when you understand this, you realize the only way out is by forgiving. Heroes rescue themselves, too.

One day, you might get to where you say, "Okay, I'll forgive them, but I won't forget!" Is that forgiving? Really?

This is where reconstructing your set comes in. *Intentional* reconstructing, really.

Actually, forgiveness doesn't mean forgetting. It has more to do with accepting a different view of what happened. It has to do with understanding. It has to do with compassion. And it has to do with seeing the benefit of forgiving, getting over it, and getting on with life.

How long do you want to suffer and give yourself ulcers, or colitis, or frazzled nerves? You're doing it, not anyone else.

No doubt, there have been horrible things done to people. But take a look at the options and the ramifications of each response. You can respond angrily, which may be absolutely appropriate, and you can deal with it and let it go.

There are so many things unknown. There are so many bigger plans, and bigger pictures of which we have no idea. We just do the best we can. We rage; we grieve; we blame.

Hopefully, in times of loss, we come to understand the lessons we can learn, and appreciate what we had for the short time we had it.

Time can bury pain, but not heal pain. Forgiveness heals pain. Forgive, and have some compassion. Then you can heal. Then you can escape from the trap, and build a more actor-friendly set. Build it with intention – to be free of the blame trap.

Once the set is built, the stage can be set.

From the director's chair:
When you give a gift, are you giving a gift or making a deal?
Who do you blame? For what?
Is it time to forgive them and stop blaming?
How could you find compassion and/or understanding for those you blame?

Setting The Stage

Every day, you get an opportunity to set the stage, position the cameras, and select the lens to use for the shot.

Every day, you have a chance to observe what works for you, and what doesn't. And every day, there is a chance to modify the stage to make things more in line with what you want for yourself, and, perhaps, your world.

Imagine this scene: there is a garden in the North where

great vegetables are planted. But no citrus fruit trees. No palm trees. No cactus. Only what can grow in the North is planted.

In the South, a great orchard is filled with citrus trees, bearing fruit year after year. But the orchard contains no cranberries, or blueberries. It is filled with only what can grow in the South.

Nature dictates what grows where. Planting palm trees in the North would be a bad idea.

When setting the stage, set it with intention, selecting scenery and props that reflect your priorities and desires. Listen to what you hear inside.

There is a vibration, ever-present, that hums like a divine machine, and it purrs everywhere, including in you. If you listen in stillness, it can be heard. It's energy. It's part of Nature.

Man may be the only creature capable of attempting to overrule Nature. It can't be done, of course, but man is arrogant enough or ignorant enough to try.

The way Nature has set the stage, the river flows one way. Swimming upstream, like planting palms in the North, is so difficult. It's exhausting. And why even try, when there is a natural current available to take you to amazing places you haven't even dreamed of?

And Nature has cast everyone with talents. Every living human being is good at many things. Why not use what you've been given? Why not do something that utilizes your natural talents? Why not do what resonates within? Why not live naturally?

You could call it *Intentional Living*, that is, to be the way you would like the world to be. If you would like the world to be peaceful, then think, speak, and act peacefully. If you would like others to treat you honestly, then think, speak, and act honestly. If you prefer kindness, then be kind. Whatever is put out in the world must come back. It's impossible to work differently. It's a law of Nature. It's cause and effect.

Whenever man acts with no regard for Nature, Nature places a wake-up call. "Hello. This isn't a good idea. Wake up and learn."

Everything we need as a species is here. The stage has been set divinely. All sorts of delicious food for sustenance; plenty of natural material for shelter and clothing; colorful beauty for joy any time you choose to connect with it; medicines and cures for health; even mineral resources for endless uses. And it's all natural.

But some insist on resetting the stage! They are the ones who are processing foods, using synthetic materials with chemicals for shelter and clothing, replacing the natural beauty with artificial landscapes, manufacturing medicines with side effects, and overusing so many minerals while ignoring natural alternatives.

There is so much to learn. The pace of life is so fast. The quick, short-term options seem so convenient and harmless and economical. So often, trial and error rules. The challenge is to see the errors, not repeat them.

One day, this will all change, and man will choose what Nature provides. Or the hero will fall.

From the director's chair:
What are you naturally good at?
How could you use your natural talents more?
How could you behave in ways you'd like others
to behave more often?
What are some new ways to approach old problems?

The Curtain Rises

As the curtain rises, there is a split screen. On the left, children are playing. They express themselves naturally. They share, or they don't share. They cry when they are upset. They laugh when they're happy.

On the right of the screen, adults are arguing. Over money. Over love. Over rules. Over words. They express in learned ways. They blame. They deceive. They use power. They force. They act out of fear. They intimidate. They act out of guilt. They stuff their feelings. They don't let on whenever they're afraid or unsure. They hide, lie, worry, and resent.

One scene leads to another in life. And in Nature. In choices. In thoughts. In actions. In feelings. Like chapters in a book, like floors in a building, and, yes, like scenes in a movie.

In the beginning, before school restricted them, before parents scolded them, before society spurned them, Dick and Jane were pure, natural children.

While some supported and encouraged them, others

infected them. "What's wrong with you!" "You should be ashamed of yourself!" "Stop crying!" Be quiet!" "No!" "No!" "No!"

Here's how the scenes unfolded after their Purity (I am) was infiltrated by shame (there's something wrong with me): Their shame led to sadness (there's something wrong with me that I can't fix), which led to anger (I'm flawed and I'm helpless!), which led to blame (it must be someone else's fault), which led to separation (I'm different), which led to fear (I'll always be different), which led to denial (I'll pretend I'm not different), which led to illness (I'm a fake and it makes me sick), which led to treatment (my symptoms can be fixed), which led to progress (I feel better), which led to hope (I can get well), which led to light (I can see something bright), which led to good (I like this), which led to health (all systems are go!), which led to balance (everything is steady), which led to peace (everything is), which led to Purity (I am).

So, Dick and Jane find happiness, but not before getting sick, because symptoms get treated. There is no prescription for prevention.

How does a shamed child not grow up and pass shame on to his or her offspring when he or she has been so programmed? How can a new, healthy environment/scene be created? The first step, of course, is awareness of the situation, and the second is the courage to break the chain.

Jack was the son of an alcoholic, who was the son of an alcoholic. For years he was a victim, losing jobs, relationships, and money. But somehow, he found the courage to do something about it, as many have. He sought help. He took back control of his life. He broke the chain.

You have to know that you have the power to break it. The option is always there. You *always* have the option, but it takes vision, and will, and courage.

In the movie of your life, can you be the hero or heroine who has the courage to break the cycle? Can you see ahead to what the next ten or twenty years of scenes will look like if you don't break the cycle? Can you see those scenes if you do break it? Which movie is yours?

As sure as night follows day, every cycle will end. Every chain will be broken.

On the pain/pleasure continuum, there is a section I call the Valley of Complacency, where the pain hurts, but it is tolerable. No action is taken here, until the pain increases sufficiently or the *carrot* of pleasure appears rewarding enough.

Jack undoubtedly got to a point where the pain became intolerable, and he had to act. He had to do something, even surrender.

The question, then, becomes "Will the Good Guy step forward?"

From the director's chair:
How would each step of the Purity cycle apply to you?
In what area(s) of life are you in the Valley of Complacency?
What would the scenes look like ten years from now if you stay there?
What carrot would cause you to act?

Go For The Love

(Lyrics by Peter Schroeder)

Quiet your thoughts. Breathe in the calming air.
Ask for the guidance. Listen and wait.
If you are to love, be open and freely live,
You first of all must forgive, to unlock the gate.

You hold on to pain, refusing to drop the charge.
But you are the captive, imprisoned inside.
Let it all go. You'll never know peace until
You shift your perspective, dispose of your pride.

Go For The Love, love unconditional
Let go of torment, of sad memory.
You have things to do. Get on with the journey now.
The gate is before you, and you hold the key.

What is our world, when looked at through loving eyes?
See everyone trying the best that they can.
How can one judge? How can one criticize?
How can one be anything but part of the plan?

Go For The Love, love unconditional.
Let your heart open. Let yourself free.
You have things to do. Get on with the journey now.
The gate is before you, and you hold the key.

2

Establishing Conflict

The Good Guy Stumbles
Villains & Props
Special Effects
I Can Choose

The Good Guy Stumbles

You've read books and seen films about the perfect crime; heard the talk about a perfect game, and seen ads for the perfect gift. Well, here's a little story about the Perfect Mistake.

I know it well because I had been making the Perfect Mistake for more years than I care to remember.

The hard truth is that in order to personally learn anything, there must be challenges. They become lessons. You have to stumble, then rise. Like toddlers stumble many times before they can walk across a room. And the subplots that teach lessons can be painful.

I had learned early on that people around me would be happy (read: love me) if I behaved. And I learned early on that if I didn't behave, I'd have unhappy people around – namely, my parents. They might yell at me, or send me to my room, or get out the hairbrush. (Ouch!)

I was little and they were the parents, the grown-ups, the directors of life. I now know they were doing the best they could.

They were training me to obey the rules, to be able to please people (yes, I became a people-pleaser), and not to embarrass them.

As an adult, I carried these messages deeply in my brain somewhere. And I became quite adept, I thought, at not just pleasing people, but making their day. Being a bright spot in their week. And I admit I still have some remains of those beliefs.

However (finally), after many years, I have learned the hard, hard way that, lo and behold, I am not perfect. I can't please all of the people all of the time. In fact, I have come to accept the concept that no matter how I behave, some people won't like me, and many people won't care. And of course some will love me, even when I'm me, not trying to be something I'm not.

In an inspired moment, I let go of the notion of having to be perfect in order to earn love. I even saw the beauty in not trying to be perfect. Instead, I assumed a much easier and realistic role of being as honest and kind as I could be, and let those closest to me know of my revised priorities. Imagine what a huge relief that was! I no longer felt compelled to try to be perfect.

I quickly experienced how much more energy I had. How much had I given to that insane attempt at perfection? It was truly hopeless.

On the other hand, the path I had traveled led me to where I now find myself, with much learned on the way. Could I have done it differently, less painfully? I am very satisfied saying I don't know.

Celebrities, with all their packaging, with all their success, get verbally slammed by some critics and the public on a daily basis. Even movie stars know *you'll never please 'em all.*

I believe we are perfectly divine. I believe we are holy, perfect expressions of love and light. Nature is perfect, and we are part of Nature. And, try as we may to be someone else, we are who we are.

So, you be you. This is exactly where making your own movie comes in. Discover what's important to you, what rings true for you. And write your script according to those principles and convictions.

Why not write a role for yourself that lets you be you, warts and all? Not only is it the best way to tackle the villains that undoubtedly will show up, but it's an easier and more comfortable part to play, and your movie will be more fulfilling and rewarding.

From the director's chair:
Are you a people-pleaser?
Who loves you no matter what you do?
How would you spend an entire day being completely you?
Could you try it and not be attached to what other people think?

Villains & Props

Movie villains come in many forms. You've seen monsters, insects, criminals, and politicians. For a hero to be a hero, a villain is absolutely necessary.

And to overcome obstacles and grow, there must be obstacles.

One of the cleverest villains ever encountered is the human mind. It can connive, cajole, and convince. What's a hero to do?

This is where props come in handy. So, choose the props that help subdue the villains. Just as Luke Skywalker has his Light Sabre, and Harry has magic, you, too, have a special prop.

At your disposal is a unique switch – The Past/Future Switch! Unfortunately, if this switch has been neglected, then you've stayed stuck in the past, repeating painful tendencies all too often. But now, as a brilliant and resourceful hero, you can use this prop, this Past/Future Switch, for your own good.

When you flip the Switch, you can instantly flip from gloom to hope. It applies direct power to transform your outlook, which, actually, is quite amazing.

Rebecca had a common track record – one bad relationship after another. She had no problem meeting men, she just kept choosing men she thought she could "rescue," and ended up getting hurt. It took a courageous friend to talk with her and point out this habitual behavior. The role she had created for herself, the rescuer, was unrealistic and unfair.

The guys didn't want or ask to be rescued, and she was spending years playing an impossible role. Then, her friend stepped in. She painted a clear picture of the cycle, and Rebecca understood. It didn't take her long to approach her next relationship with no pretense of rescuing anybody, except herself!

And to no one's surprise, that's the relationship which is lasting to this day. Her perspective of the past served as a guide for her. She actually has come to be grateful for those dead-ends, as she realized they taught her a valuable lesson. They weren't dead-ends, just stepping stones.

When *It's Your Movie!*, this is the key to the whole concept! The events of the past are unchangeable, but (this is one of those **BIG** buts) you can, at any time, change your meaning of, or response to, a situation. You can add insight to anything that happened in the past. Simply flip the Switch!

Flip the Switch to avoid repeating bad habits, dead-end patterns, and unfulfilling trends. Even generational, inherited attitudes and tendencies can be altered with commitment and a shift in perspective.

Then you can stop dwelling on regrets, resentments, and "mistakes." Remembrances of past events can shift into helpful lessons, rather than unhealthy sources of pain.

Close your eyes, take a few slow, deep breaths, and ask in what area of life you are stuck in the past, what area needs to be re-examined. Ask your inner, intuitive wisdom for suggestions on how to initiate any beneficial changes.

The river of life flows. You can constantly experience and learn new things. Attitudes periodically evolve; priorities are not what they used to be. And they will not remain "as is" forever.

Everything is in motion. The past does not have to equal the future.

Once the Past/Future Switch has been flipped, and you realize the past is not necessarily the future, you can assess the situation and discover what yearns to be modified or rewritten most. Then start writing the role of your dreams!

It's Your Movie! You are the star *and* the screenwriter! Write yourself a dynamic character, one who learns as he or she goes on, encountering interesting adventures, and enjoying memorable moments of connection, purpose, and satisfaction. Write as though it will make a difference in your life.

Every day, you wake up, only and always, to today. Yesterday is always completely over; learn from it. Today awaits you. And tomorrow, you will write more.

This day is yours for the taking. Grab it. Seize it, as they say, and "write" the day and the life you want. You hold the pen. And now you have found the Switch. So, use this prop to conquer the villains!

From the director's chair:
What old habits hold you back? How?
What new behaviors, in line with your priorities,
could replace them?
How did it feel to write a new script?
What would happen if you made those scenes part of your movie?

Special Effects

Now that the villain has been cast, and a great prop has been discovered, let's wow 'em with some special effects! With the technology of today, special effects are included in almost every film. They allow the filmmaker to create illusions that convince the audience the hero is hanging from a cliff, or the aliens have taken the shape of kiwi fruit.

Of course, life is full of its own special effects – things that appear real but are totally figments of the imagination.

Always, they are caused by the ego. For the ego likes to make so many things seem true and good for you. Here are a few:

- instant gratification
- you'll be safe if you hide and stay in your own little comfort zone
- you'll feel better if you put others down
- those regrets will be around forever
- life isn't fair
- be afraid

And on. And on. And on.

Fear resides in the ego, as do vanity and shame. The ego says *lie*, and it justifies the lies in the name of protection. It can cause intimidation in the same way it can instill confidence, because the ego says people are different from you – they are better or worse than you, to be feared or loved.

Ego creates separation. And then it find things to prove the story is true. It's a real self-fulfilling prophecy.

My wife and I used to have a house on the shore of a

small lake. I loved living by the water. Each day, it was as though it had a certain mood, and I found it to be a great plus in my life.

That lake was really a wide spot in a river. The dam kept the lake at the desired level, so our yard never flooded, and it never completely froze up in the winter. A couple thousand geese loved it enough to occupy the unfrozen part each year, and we enjoyed watching them and listening to them communicate. Some neighbors found them annoying. Imagine that!

We had a deck where we'd sit and have some meals, entertain friends, and produce some wonderful memories. I'd sit and write out there quite often.

One day, a pretty good breeze was blowing, and the water got wavy, of course. From right to left, as I looked, the waves were moving fast. Somehow, it occurred to me that the current was moving, even at that very moment, from left to right.

And then it struck me that on the surface, while all the forces were conspiring to move that water in one direction, the current, the deep force that never needed to conspire, was still doing its job, still moving the deep water, in the direction it was meant to move.

I thought of my ego, and life's distractions, enticing me, seducing me to move in a direction contrary to my deep convictions and principles. I thought of how the water had no choice, but I could always determine the way I moved. I thought of how the ego can be so loud, so strong, so sensible. I thought of how the quiet voice that never shouts can be temporarily unheard because of the big wind that is my ego-voice.

My wife and I were paddling a canoe on a river in northern Wisconsin once, against the wind, and I assured her that the return trip would be easier because we'd be going with the wind. Well, when we turned around, that wind must have snickered as it died down. We ended up paddling against the current on the way back. It was a long trip.

There are illusions in life. These are the special effects, created by the ego to protect, but more often than not, they keep some beautiful dream from coming true. Often these special effects come in the form of fears. Or limitations. Or character traits.

Some fears are healthy – being afraid of sunburn, for example, which prompts the use of sunscreen. Some limits are healthy – not lifting more than you think you can handle. Some traits are healthy – confidence to try something new.

As you learn about these special effects, you can get to the real nitty-gritty of life. You can get a clearer picture of what you're here to learn. You can even learn to better distinguish the true from the false. Listen for that voice that resonates within. That's no special effect!

But remember, the special effects are definitely there for good reasons. What would a movie be without them?

From the director's chair:

What special effects does your ego try to make you believe are real?
How do they go against your deeper sense of truth?
What fears, limitations, and traits have you made up?
What can you do to eliminate or replace them?

I Can Choose

(Lyrics by Peter Schroeder)

I watch the water on the lake, as it's pushed on by the wind.
It seems to move against the current down below.
Just like my ego tries to make, to make me move, it's like that wind.
But then my heart, it whispers softly, what I should know.

I Can Choose. I can decide.
What I do. Where I go. And how I feel inside.
Because within me, there is a power, that I can use.
I Can Choose. I have a choice.
Yes, I do. Yes, I know. Inside I hear a voice.
Unlike the water on the lake, I Can Choose.

Sometimes it seems, I'm not awake, like I'm enticed on by that wind.
At times I stumble and I struggle, yet I know,
If but a moment I will take, to realize it's that ego-wind.
I must let go and be carried by the flow.

The universe is flowing,
It's never, ever still.
Our intentions are always showing,
They are reflections of our will.

You do not have to fight now,
You know you do not have to strain.
Be guided in your flight now,
I'll say it once again:

Just watch the water on the lake, as it's pushed on by the wind.
It seems to move against the current down below.
Just like our ego tries to make, to make us move, it's like that wind.
We must let go and be carried by the flow.

I Can Choose. I can decide.
What I do. Where I go. And how I feel inside.
Because within me, there is a power, that I can use.
I Can Choose. I have a choice.
Yes, I do. Yes, I know. Inside I hear a voice.
Unlike the water on the lake, I Can Choose.

3

Protagonist Emerging

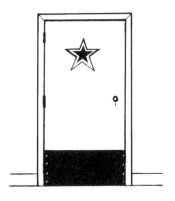

The Hero Hears A Voice
The New Camera Angle
What's My Motivation?
I Drive A Little Slower

The Hero Hears A Voice

"Use The Force, Luke!"

It might be a voice. It might be a feeling. But it's there. Some things, you just know. No one has to tell you. You don't have to see it or touch it. You just know it in your gut.

You've had these feelings from time to time. Sensations you simply know are true, at least for you.

I don't mean things like the law of gravity, or two plus two is four. I mean stuff that has a resonance within that says, "Yes. This is real." Or "I should do this, and not do that."

It's a wonderful thing, this resonance. It's like a compass that can be used as a guide. It never fails. It always knows True North.

When making your movie, employ this guidance system to discern between the ego-wants and the deeper alternatives. Choose based on how the options resonate.

Give some serious thought to what's most important to you. This internal guidance is the best resource available in this thought process, this type of discovery. And it's there to be used.

I'm sure you've had experiences where some voice inside whispered or shouted a warning to stay away from someone, or a certain situation. And you've had a feeling in your heart that connected you instantly to some stranger, or a job, or a place.

Some call this Intuition. Some refer to it as the Sixth Sense. Whatever the name, its gifts are priceless. And it's free and available, whenever you choose to use it.

There is book knowledge; there is common sense. But, I'm speaking of Sixth Sense Knowledge – Heart Knowledge. It can be used, trusted, and appreciated.

Take a minute to experiment the next time you're faced with a decision that requires some thought. Instead of thinking, try this…

Close your eyes, take some slow, deep breaths, and be still. Ask for the best options to show themselves in a way you can understand, and consider how each possibility resonates within. Distinguish the one that hits home. Then, confidently follow your gut. Decide, believing and trusting that Sixth Sense Knowledge knows best.

A good director listens to his Sixth Sense. He has a feel for who can play a role, where to put the cameras, and who to hire as assistants. He trusts his gut. Alfred Hitchcock knew exactly where to put the cameras, how to use the lighting to get the look he wanted. It was his instinctive decisions that set him apart.

A good writer knows when he's ready to let the words come forth. He's in touch with his unconscious talent for expressing his story in perfect detail. He's willing to rely on himself and the resources at his disposal to best convey everything he wishes, in the precise manner which has become his style.

Nicholas Sparks, author of "Message in a Bottle," says

he knows when he's heading in the wrong direction with a plot – he gets writer's block. On his website, he explains that he pays attention to this signal and stops moving forward; he goes back over what he's written and corrects the problem. He listens to his gut.

A good actor knows how to deliver what the character demands by trusting his gut. Being technically correct isn't enough. His unique flavor is what makes the difference, and nails the scene.

Ingrid Bergman said it best: "You must train your intuition – you must trust the small voice inside you which tells you exactly what to say, what to decide."

So, listen for that Inner Voice. Feel the vibration. Learn to recognize the resonance that can guide you to become all that you are. It's there.

Make it a regular practice to get in touch with it. Use that Inner Voice for as many things as possible, in as many ways as you want. See firsthand how life can become so much easier and so much more rewarding.

It's up to you. It's always your choice. It's always your movie. You can even let that voice lead you to a new camera angle.

From the director's chair:
When have you heard that voice, guiding you as you made a decision?
When have you trusted it and what was the result?
What happened when you heard it, but you went against it?
How could you use the voice right now to help you make a decision?

The New Camera Angle

Hitchcock was the master at picking precisely the right shot to set up the scene. His camera angles contributed greatly to the overall feel of his movies. And he wasn't afraid to opt for the unexpected.

One of the most amazing insights I've ever experienced came in the most unexpected way.

I was at a workshop with my wife and part of the workshop had to deal with anger. I really don't get angry very often, at least not externally. So, I was approaching this exercise thinking I could observe others and that would be it.

The night before the anger part of the workshop, we were not supposed to talk with others, so as to stay within our own thoughts, and not be distracted.

Right before we were going to go to bed, my wife passed by me, on the way to brush her teeth, and she said, "Excuse me" as she passed by.

I couldn't believe it! She coerced me into going to this workshop. I really didn't want to go. (Or so I thought.) Then she goes and ruins it for me by speaking during a time when we were instructed not to talk! Unbelievable!

I must say here that I am a rather black-and-white kind of guy, in case you haven't noticed, so if the rules say no talking, that means no talking, no exceptions – those are the rules.

Now I'm furious. I'm glaring at her, but, of course, not uttering a sound. How could she?! Her little words were so unnecessary!

Next morning, I woke up early. I didn't sleep much, as you could probably guess, and was still extremely angry. I got dressed, gathered my things and left our room for the morning session of the workshop.

I arrived too early. The room was still locked and so I found a place to sit, overlooking the lake, and went over the previous night's debacle.

During this reflection, the big "aha!" occurred. Unplanned by me or my wife, I had been given the golden opportunity to access my anger, something I probably otherwise would have been unable or unwilling to do. Everyone knows anger is *bad* – so I thought at the time. But there I was, still blowing steam out of my ears, like the mad bull in the cartoons.

And as I was sitting there, I thought, "This incident didn't happen *to* me, it happened *for* me." *It happened for me!* And then I was stunned as I thought, "*Every*thing that happens, happens *for* me. Nothing happens *to* me."

That one little word change has changed my life. It's really true. It has changed my life. And things really happen for me, not to me.

Relating this to movies, every director has a choice of camera angles, or points of view. A new point of view, like the one described above, can change any scene.

Consider the possibility that everything happens *for* you, and not *to* you. And you can select a different camera angle.

When things happen to you, you are a victim. You might feel shame or that you have been unfairly treated. You may even believe you deserve to be a victim – whether the victim of an illness, an accident, or any painful situation.

But when you understand that things happen for you, you become the recipient of gifts, or lessons, that are for your benefit. That guy cutting you off reminded you to slow down. And you have a new camera angle.

That little distinction can make a huge difference. Life goes from being unfair, to being not only fair, but being a series of gifts. If you think back to a situation that seemed unfair at the time, you may actually be able to see a benefit from that incident today.

Little words can make big differences. Little shifts in perspective can take a life of despair, and give it instant hope, with no thought of fair or unfair. You can start individually, then expand it into families and communities, and finally, the world has changed.

It's a matter of camera angle. Get motivated to try a new one.

From the director's chair:
When have you had a dramatic change in an opinion or attitude? Did the change benefit you? How?
What would happen if you spent one week pretending everything happens for you?
How would your family benefit from this experiment?

What's My Motivation?

Every actor needs to know what is motivating his character. Why is the character acting in a certain way, saying certain words, expressing certain emotions? Motivation always drives the dialogue and the action.

Dynamic characters have changing or evolving motivation. Here's a close-to-home example:

There was a time, not that long ago, when I'd always drive as if I were in some kind of race. I'd play the game of getting wherever I was going, as fast as I could, weaving through traffic. It was fun.

Some time between then and now, I've started to take life a bit slower, and enjoy the trip as I go.

Things change. People change. Priorities change. And I notice these changes whenever someone comes into view who is doing things like I used to do back then.

The kids today drive just like I did. And they crank up the volume, just like I did. I smile when I encounter one of these high-flyers. I think, "Just wait, my friend. You'll lose the piercings, the tattoos, and the fast-as-I-can way of life. Or maybe you won't."

Another change is my choice of radio stations. Back in the old days, I listened to the top-40 stations that were gradually replaced by the underground FM ones that played the album cuts that AM didn't.

I'm not that into "cutting-edge" radio these days. Now, I

find talk radio interesting. What doesn't change?

The reason I'm bringing all this up is that, like everything else, motivations change. Maybe not as drastically as radio preferences, or volume levels, but important convictions and priorities certainly are areas of potential change and evolution. And motivation drives it all.

Think back a few years. How far back do you have to go before you remember thinking and believing differently about religion, or politics, or the lyrics of a song?

Recently, I heard Dylan's "The Times, They Are A-Changing," and the song got to the line about how "your sons and your daughters are beyond your command." It stopped me in my tracks! I always related to the son mentioned. This time, I related to the parent of the son! Yikes!

I definitely hear things differently. And I prioritize differently. So many changes. All the changes in my life are reflections of changes in my intentions. How about you? Go back five years. Ten years. Twenty years.

So many changes in motivation and intentions!

As you write the next scenes for your movie, give some thought as to why you make certain decisions, choose one option over another, and consider what qualities you wish to demonstrate.

You really have a broad array of choices. Just think of how you relate to your surroundings. What's your motivation for keeping them in the shape they're in? Are they the way you'd like them if a camera were going to film them for public viewing today? Maybe you're somewhat grateful that there is no camera around today. But that's just a small example of how you can use motivation to write your script.

Get clear on a motivation, and it will lead to action.

From the director's chair:

What are your primary motivators? Money? Fear? Acceptance? How have they changed over the years? What's been the biggest change?

How has your motivation led you to action?

What new motivators could stimulate you to create a more vibrant life?

I Drive A Little Slower

(Lyrics by Peter Schroeder)

I Drive A Little Slower, and I think a little more.
I listen to some stations that I never tried before.
I look around and wonder what all the rush is for.
I Drive A Little Slower and I think a little more.

I'm busier than ever. Priorities have changed.
Neighbors moved; old friends have gone; and families have rearranged.
I once had all the answers, but now I'm not so sure.
So I Drive A Little Slower and I think a little more.

What about you? What do you think?
As you listen to this little song, and stare into your drink?

Do you Drive A Little Slower? Do you think a little more?
Have you listened to some stations, you never tried before?
Do you look around and wonder what all the rush is for?
Do you Drive A Little Slower and think a little more?

Now, I'm stuck behind some grandpa, poking down this hill.
If he was going any slower, he'd be standing still.
And I can read his bumper sticker, clearly in my view:
It says "I may be slow, but I'm ahead of you."

People don't change. That's what they say.
But I'd like to talk to "them" about the way I am today.

I Drive A Little Slower, and I think a little more.
I listen to some stations that I never tried before.
I look around and wonder what all the rush is for.
I Drive A Little Slower and I think a little more.

4

Plot Twists

Non-Stop Action
Powerful Dialogue
Filming Close To Home
Fathers 'n' Sons

Non-Stop Action

The world loves action. Action-packed movies bring in the big numbers, and studios are starving for a new twist on an old theme. But whatever the subject of the film, give 'em plenty of action and they'll fill the seats.

For everyone but cloistered monks, life is filled with action. More action than you may realize. Daily action. Continuous action, like it or not. It's inevitable, because as time marches on, things change.

Change is the way. Expected, but unexpected. Maybe this sounds familiar: *Yeah, I know change is going to happen, but could it please cooperate a little more? It's just that it doesn't show up when and where I want it. In fact, I usually don't want it anyway. And the changes I want, well, they can be difficult or impossible to produce, yet the unwanted ones seem unavoidable and unstoppable.*

This is the non-stop action of life.

What is it about change that is so difficult to accept when everyone knows that things always change? Nothing stays the same forever. Yes, everyone know that, yet...

The fact is that change is not only inevitable, it's good! It's what make life interesting. It adds color and wonder and excitement to your existence. Change is part of Nature. Your challenge is to make the best of it. In your movie, your opportunity is to use it as a tool to improve the plot. Your fate is to deal with it.

Change can be initiated by you, or by someone or something else. Typically, if you start the change, it is because you want the change. Conversely, if the change is started by someone or something else, you are probably either ambivalent or you don't like or want it.

When you're making your movie, use the camera lens of choice to see the gift or lesson in any change, and influence the process by actively participating, rather than resisting. Participating (active) always means you are not a victim (passive). Participating means you are acting (literally, here) to manage the change into healthy, positive directions, like water irrigating dry lands, not sitting by as the water floods the streets and buildings.

Writing and directing with intention let you speak out against unhealthy, abusive behaviors. Changes that are proposed out of fear, or that attempt to perpetuate fear, can be seen as catalysts that encourage action. But, acts of fear countered by more acts of fear are not solutions, only postponers, of real solutions. And the movie drags on.

As the executive producer of your movie, what do you want to use as the basis for action? Love? Fear? Changes that are initiated out of love are changes that are disdained only by the fearful. Changes initiated by the fearful are changes that are contrary to Nature and cannot endure.

Ultimately, Nature has the final say in which changes last the longest, as those are the ones that work *with* Nature, not against It or oblivious to It.

There is always action. There are always changes coming down the road. The opportunity is always before you.

Prepare for the changes. Remember your priorities, convictions, and principles.

Without preparation, you are left to your knee-jerk fight or flight responses. But if you fight, can you win? If you run, can you escape?

What about another alternative that is less primitive and more intelligent? What about being pro-active? Anticipating and expecting it? Considering possibilities and preparing accordingly?

That's making a movie with real intention in mind. That's directing from a place of vision, shooting behind a camera of confidence, filming memorable scenes of struggle and redemption and powerful dialogue.

Go ahead, say it – *"Action!"*

From the director's chair:
When you act, are you moving toward a goal or desire, or away from pain or fear?
What have been the consequences of directing your lens toward fear as opposed to goals?
What changes would you most like to see in your life?
What simple thing could you do differently this week, just to notice the benefit of change?

Powerful Dialogue

While action provides visual appeal, and keeps our attention, scripting is, arguably, the most important process in making a film. The dialogue can determine the effectiveness of the entire movie.

Interestingly, linguists tell us words themselves account for but 7% of communication. The huge majority of communication depends on the tone of voice (38%) and body language (a whopping 55%).

Here's something to consider: when not face-to-face, that is, when body language is out of the equation, tone of voice zooms proportionately to approximately 84.5%, while the words make up 15.5% of communication. So that would include phone conversations, recordings like music and narratives, CDs and tapes, and all other words spoken and heard without observation. 84.5% is tone of voice. Wow! If Shakespeare didn't warn, "Actors, beware thy delivery!", he should have.

Remember this when scripting and delivering lines.

Also, remember that Nature has some undeniable laws, and one of them has to do with spoken words. It says:

Every word has rippling effects that *never go away. They exist as energy forever!*

Who hasn't spoken and heard words of support or comfort that made an impact, or words of deception or anger that have an effect, years later?

What is said always makes a difference, always has some impact, and if the same thought is expressed by many voices, that impact is increased accordingly. This can be seen in the power of prayer.

It's actually a wonderful law. It's part of the beauty of Nature. It demonstrates the truth of the substance of words. And it means you have input and participation in the way things are. This is fantastic!

Think of what this makes available to you − it gives power to your movie and your intention. It gives power to the vibrations set in motion by your very own voice.

There are literally thousands of people who have direct experience of the old adage: Be careful what you ask for . . . you might just get it.

You know someone, I guarantee it, who has asked for something they never thought possible, yet received the very thing they requested.

If you doubt this, interview a few friends, and it won't take long before one will gladly relate how they hoped to manifest something in general, or prayed specifically for some exact result, and then, at some time in the future, got what they said they wanted. If they asked in general, they received in general. If they asked specifically, they received specifically. It's simply a law of Nature.

It works because that's just the way Nature works. And if you think about it, it couldn't work any other way. It's part of what makes free will free. It's part of what goes around, comes around. It's part of Natural supply and demand.

Now here's where you have to be really extra careful:

If a thought occurs to you that is less than desirable, should it become true, do yourself a favor and let it go. Do not give it a place and a reason to manifest by saying it out loud. Replace it in your mind by some alternate, preferred thought and say that one aloud. Give *it* the power.

As ideas come that seem healthy, desirable, or empowering, speak them out loud, write them down, and make them part of your movie's dialogue.

Share them with other people. Each expression adds power. Each repetition creates more energy. Use this divine tool. The tools of Nature are always there to be utilized to help you learn more, enjoy more, and assist others more.

The power of the spoken word is there for you to accomplish whatever your intention may be. It's there whether you realize it or not. Just as hearts beat automatically, intentions are always present, whether you are aware of them or not. And words have power, whether you comprehend it or not.

There exists an unbreakable connection between intentions and words. If you try to deceive or mislead, by saying one thing when your intention is something else, then the wheel starts to spin, and you will experience the consequences. It never fails! It can't fail – it's a law of Nature.

So choose your words wisely, speak sweetly, and deliver them with care, not because you may have to eat your words, but because you *surely* will have to sleep in the bed you make, and eat your words, too! Got that, you princes of Hollywood, you princesses of Sundance?

With your intentional script in hand, it's time to consider locations. With so much of the action in your life, and so much of the dialogue taking place there, you can't help but include scenes filmed right in your own back yard.

From the director's chair:

What words from the past do you remember? Are they painful or pleasing?

What words do you regret? What words do you wish you would have said?

Where in your life do your words not match your convictions and ideals?

What words can you add to your script that will give you more power?

Filming Close To Home

When parts of a film are shot close to home, the script is easy to write because the roles in homes are meted out more or less automatically. But as there have been scores of movies about doomed relationships and dysfunctional families, the real world "automatically" succumbs to social pressures, just like the fictional plots on the big screen.

When you're making your movie, you owe it to yourself, and generations to come, to do everything in your power to keep these pressures from silently stealing control, and joy.

There has evolved in our culture a deeply damaging set-up. The mother has for decades, if not centuries, been the nurturer and caretaker of the family; while the father has been the breadwinner and the provider. As you know, it is now more common than not that the mother works outside the home while doing her best to fulfill the nurturing and caretaking responsibilities.

The father has been guided by society to spend more time away from the house. Business travel and pressure find him gone more than ever, emotionally if not physically.

The daughters have the mother around to observe and emulate. Where does that leave the sons? Who do they look up to? With whom can they develop a male bond?

Undoubtedly, you don't have to look far from your neighborhood to find a situation that embodies this set-up.

Overall, the importance of fathers in our culture has been grossly misunderstood and consequently undervalued, with ramifications that damage not only individuals and families, but all of society.

With no role for the father in raising the children, a tilted relationship is formed between the children and each parent. The mother is much too close, with too many responsibilities, and the father is too distant, with too few responsibilities.

Families with strong father-figures grow responsible, balanced children with high self-esteem, who live healthy lives. Where there are weak or in-absentia father-figures, the sons are confused about how a man fits in. There are two strikes against him as he becomes an adult.

This is not to say great citizens cannot be raised in single-parent homes – many are, no doubt. However, it's a tough road for all involved.

This may get worse before it gets better, for society is slow to react to most social problems. But we are too intelligent a race to ignore it. Eventually, we must come to realize that a father is necessary, valuable, and deserving of a respected place in the family unit.

As you make your movie, is your conscious awareness sensitive enough to pick up on the whispers and screams of our sons and our fathers, and the desperate pleas of our daughters and mothers? Will it become part of the collective consciousness? Who will feel compelled to act, to spread the word, to alert others of the danger?

Who will shout out, *"**Sons, have compassion for your father. Fathers, reach out and express your love to your boys. Don't put it off. Start today. Be part of the solution.**"*?

Like everyone else, you are part masculine and part feminine. Whether male or female, you have some capability to nurture, as well as to provide. This world is shared by all of civilization, to have and to hold, for better or for worse, for richer, for poorer, in sickness and in health, from this day forward till death do us part.

Perhaps pain and dysfunction can't be written out entirely, but a concerted effort can be made, starting in the home, to honor the roles of men and women, and their place in their family's movie.

Our movie, the Big Movie, the one we're all in, as we now find it, is our making. It is ours to correct as we see fit. We each play our roles, and speak our lines. The relationships and dynamics between the characters develop more fully. And we live in the result, close to home.

From the director's chair:

What role did you assign your father? Your mother?
Have you taken on your father's role? Your mother's role?
How have these choices impacted other parts of your life?
What would you need to do to expand your role?

Fathers 'n' Sons

(Lyrics by Peter Schroeder)

Hey son, don't cry.
Demons 'n' monsters will soon be gone.
Hey son, don't cry.
Blue skies 'n' sunshine be comin' on.
Mama will comfort you, you know.
Mama will nurture you, for sure.
That's what mamas are for.
And as for me...

Father, don't cry.
Pain 'n' sorrow will soon be gone.
Father, don't cry.
Blue skies 'n' sunshine be comin' on.
Daughter will comfort you, you know.
Daughter will nurture you, for sure.
That's what daughters are for.
And as for me...

Father, don't die.
So many things that I gotta say.
Father, don't die.
I ain't ready to face that day.
Let me try to comfort you, you know.
Let me try to do my best, for sure.
Let me try to open that door
'Tween you 'n' me.

5

Hope

Sharing The Lead
Defining The Roles
Expanding The Cast
The Family I Love

Character Development

As roles are assigned, and characters develop along the story's path, a beautiful emergence takes place. Encouraged by the supporting characters, the lead demonstrates depth.

In fact, only the relationships with the others can bring out the lead's qualities, and he or she grows more endearing. This is how the lead gets to be the personality he or she is. Watch how the lead interacts with the supporting actors, and learn the real character.

The Godfather movie is a perfect example of this. Notice how Don Corleone relates with his sons, his wife, how he treats his enemies. This is how his true personality emerges. A well-written film allows the lead to reveal himself by his actions and interactions.

So, this is about being fully expressive in your world, in your movie, as you've created it. This is about an intentional path to simple, joyful living.

No doubt, you've experienced times when you've been engaged in some activity or circumstance when you felt perfectly cast, using your natural talents, so effortlessly being who you are meant to be, that time flew by, and after, you felt completely fulfilled, useful, and worthwhile. There were no distractions, worries, nor problems.

Everyone has experienced these times in different settings. Some might have been involved with a large group of people; some may have been all alone; some could have been with one other person. The options were varied, yet there were absolute similarities in what happened.

When you are in this state of pure being, there really are no feelings, nor conscious moments of time. You are totally consumed by the activity. The focus is one-dimensional. Concentration is effortless.

If you were to recall one or several of these times in your own life, and observe and identify various factors from those times, with regard to details such as surroundings, activities, and your role in the scene, you would discover something highly useful. You would discover your natural role in life! And this role is your key to joy!

That role is simply the description of your relationship to others, regardless of what was going on. How would you describe the *function* of the character? Here are a few examples to get you started:

- teacher
- supporter
- organizer
- teammate
- designer
- leader
- motivator
- mentor

Each of these is someone *in relation* to someone else. There is always a relationship involved. The beauty here is that once you have clearly identified that relationship, you can then replicate that role, that relationship, as often as you like. Keep in mind that while several roles may seem to fit, there is always one that lets you be more expressive and fulfilled than others. Think "fulfilled" to ascertain the most genuine role.

Let's say your role is that of a Motivator. Now that you know that, you can devise or revise (write) areas of your life (movie) that put you in the role of Motivator. The more opportunities you can create where you get to *motivate*, at work or at home, the more you'll be expressing your true nature, and you'll be living intentionally.

This is your most important casting assignment. It can truly mean the difference between joy or misery, satisfaction or frustration. The clearer the definition of your natural role, the more rewarding your life.

Then, you can examine the roles of others in your life. Like they say in the airplane when the yellow mask comes down, "Secure yourself first, then help others."

From the director's chair:
In your life today, what are your predominant functions?
When have you been most fully you, engaged in your most natural talents?
How would you best describe these talents?
How could you use these talents more often in various areas of your life?

Defining The Roles

Some time ago, my wife remarked about how families always grow. Through weddings and births, the number of people closest to us expands and we find ourselves loving more and more sweet, precious human beings. Our family has certainly grown over the years.

We have a lot of exes in our family, too. Ex-spouses, and ex-in-laws. By the grace of God and our sincere intention, we all seem to get along. We share holidays and birthdays together, and we seem to share a common intention concerning harmony after divorce.

To be sure, there are deaths and divorces, and some disagreements can turn bitter. All in all, quite a bit of changing and rearranging. Close friends turn into family. And blood relatives lose touch. So, families evolve naturally. And this is a good thing.

As a child, I liked the storytellers in our family. In my memory, grandfathers and uncles seemed to be the best. I remember Uncle Bill telling about the time he and my aunt traveled to Sweden to visit her relatives. When they arrived, and went to pick up their rented car, he was seriously amazed that "all they had were foreign cars!"

Dad told stories about being in the Philippines during WWII, and having a pet monkey. He loved being a Marine, and regularly manages to express his belief that everyone should serve their country in the armed forces for at least a year, in some capacity. And then he also declares how he abhors war, and feels we have no business where we don't belong.

My wife and her sisters love memories of kitchens full of good smells and stories about "the old days." Their nieces and daughters would listen with big eyes as the adults reminisced of days and people gone by.

Think back to when you were young. How big was the family then? What role did everyone fill? And how about the family now? Who fills what roles? Were they assigned by matriarchs and patriarchs, or was individual intention involved? How have the roles changed over the years?

Today, my wife and I fill certain roles in our family. We have the chance to imbed in our children, nieces, and nephews suggestions they can carry with them throughout their lives. And, to be sure, we marvel at "the kids today," and how we can learn from them.

As you're making your movie, see families as sources of great joy and important lessons. Family members are so often the most available teachers. And there are no certificates necessary!

My mom loved to play games. While she liked to win, she really loved competing. She found great enjoyment in many things in life because she made a game out of them. And my dad loves to get my brothers and me to ask questions, and to always try our best at anything and everything.

I know that I have developed into the person I am largely because of what I took from my parents. And I am so grateful!

How times change! How families grow! How fascinating they can be! It's where roles become defined and redefined. And the cast can be expanded indefinitely.

From the director's chair:

What is your role in your family? How has it evolved over the years?

How do you feel about your role? How has it limited you? Helped you?

What would it take to change it, if you wanted to? What would it look like?

What family members influenced and affected your role? How?

Expanding The Cast

Movies can become more interesting as characters are added to the plot, and subplots are developed. And as roles and subplots are added, there are conflicts that arise, even as alliances are formed.

The challenges in the plot need resolution. The hero leads the charge, of course, but more often than not, the good guy and his allies band together to save the day.

Any alliance starts by one person reaching out to another, saying either "Join me," "Help me," or "May I help you?" This, then, expands into many helping many as the cast expands to face the challenges confronting them.

Life, too, is full of challenges, to be sure. And alliances

can play a big role in dealing with life's problems, whether social or personal.

National charities are perfect examples of people helping people. Chapters form in different cities and towns, and everyone gets to be generous, which makes them feel good, and the recipients are better off because of the generosity.

Support groups serve individuals across the country and around the world. 12-step groups are wonderfully popular, bringing huge changes in people's lives.

The idea of community is so underused in society! It seems that only when conditions become crises do people join forces. More often than not, do you tend to stick with those you know? Are you even a bit afraid of what lies out there?

But, just to go out into the world is a brave act, especially for a hero who feels unsafe or separate or sad or embarrassed. That takes a ton of courage. And courage, after all, is what makes a hero.

Yet, wonderful adventures and relationships lie out there, if you only give them a chance to come to light. Venturing out will add interest to a mundane movie, and excitement to a predictable plot.

You can, as an individual or with a group, take that step and be the first to extend a hand, offer a smile or a word of encouragement or compassion.

What would stop you from being the first to ask, "How can I help you?" or "Are you doing okay?"

Collectively, there exists an untapped synergy that can

propel all people toward living in peace and harmony. Individuals will always have differences, but to be accepted and loved are basic needs. Who doesn't desire safety for their children? Everyone needs the opportunity to earn their way, to use their natural talents, to contribute, and to be recognized for their contribution.

Someone has to be first. And that hero will be the someone who makes it part of their role. All it takes is vision and courage – the courage to be first.

Why not be the first to smile, be the first to say enthusiastically, "Good morning. Have a great day!" These are scenes that could pop up often in anyone's movie. And who would benefit by such frequency?

Really, what have you got to lose by reaching out and honoring the natural connection that exists at some deep level anyway? You and I share the same air, see the same sun and moon, and have the same vibrations going through us. How could anyone say that we aren't connected?

There is really nothing to lose but our fear! There is so much more to lose by prolonging the separation, and extending the fear. Staying in that safe, yet limiting life, may keep things undisturbed and you disconnected, but there is another option – one that offers untold rewards. Think of what you (and your movie) stand to gain by just a smile! And a smile can lead to an ally. And with a few allies, who knows what can be accomplished!

What would it take to reach out; to be a leader in the world; to be a courageous one; to be a visionary who can see the huge good to come from such a tiny act?

The more allies, that is, the bigger the cast of characters – think: Cecil B. DeMille! – the more interesting the movie, and the bigger the smiles on everyone's faces.

Think of all the people, all the lives you can touch, if you just step back, take a look at life from a wider angle, and consider the Long Shot.

From the director's chair:

What would you gain by being the first to approach another?
How could you expand your community?
What would you have to do?
How would you and your community benefit?

The Family I Love
(Lyrics by Peter Schroeder)

Those were the days I'll always remember.
Those are the memories I'm fondest of.
They live in my soul like a warm glowing ember.
Each year brings more to The Family I Love.

It seems long ago, there were only a few then,
Grandmas and Grandpas and of course Mom and Dad.
The family was small, but the days that I knew then
Were full of big hugs and smiles. Good times we had.

Then cousins came, and sisters and brothers -
More people to play with, and summers of fun.
Everyone laughed when we'd visit each other,
Magical days when the whole world was young.

Those were the days I'll always remember.
Those are the people I'm fondest of.
They live in my soul like a warm glowing ember.
Each year brings more to The Family I Love.

Suddenly there was a change in the weather.
I noticed the leaves on the trees start to fall.
It never occurred to me life's not forever.
A loss in the family is the hardest of all.

She passed in the summer. The days they were hollow.
The laughter fell silent, but the family survived.
And time marches on, and others would follow.
While some people said goodbye, newcomers arrived.

Those were the days I'll always remember.
Those are the memories I'm fondest of.
They live in my soul like a warm glowing ember.
Each year brings change to The Family I Love.

There's one other thing that needs to be mentioned.
On special occasions, when wedding bells chime,
We open our hearts to welcome new loved ones,
As part of the family, forever in time.

All over this land, across the wide ocean,
We've spread out in number and increased in size.
Our grandparents' smiles and grandchildren's laughter
They all blend together now, when I close my eyes.

And these are the days I'll always remember.
These are the people I'm fondest of.
They live in my soul like a warm glowing ember.
Each year brings more to The Family I Love.

6

The Climax

The Long Shot
The Close-Up
The Payoff
Let Out The Joy

The Long Shot

Long Shots are so very useful! They let the audience see a bigger picture. They put things in perspective. They serve a unique purpose by giving the director many options to move his camera – from the long shot, to a medium shot, to zoom in on a close-up – as he wishes.

As you are forming your movie, plan the close-ups by first examining the long shots.

Think of all the people who have influenced you at various times in your life. They could be friends or relatives, neighbors or colleagues. They may be people who don't even know you. But you've watched them, or read them, or heard them. And they have made an impression. They have contributed to your development, your growth, your maturity, or your wisdom. They have left a lasting mark.

Well, the reverse is just as true. There are large numbers of people who have observed *you*. Really large numbers, *every day*! People you don't know, as well as those you're very close to. All these people, collectively, form your Circle Of Influence, and they are all in your long shot.

Here's a little exercise:

Take a normal sheet of paper, and draw a big circle on it. Make it as big as you can. In the center of it, write the first names of those you are closest to. Now, spiraling outward, write the first names of your closest friends and relatives, then other friends and relatives, then neighbors, then co-workers, acquaintances, and people you barely know. Keep writing!

Think of all the shops and stores you frequent. Think of anyone you can. If you know their first name, write it in the circle. If you don't know their first name, write a brief description, so you will know who you mean.

You will easily be able to fill the circle with names. This is your personal long shot – your Circle Of Influence. These are the lives you touch, whether you know it or not. Intentionally or not.

I did this very thing when I quit my job several years ago, and started playing music at clubs. In my guitar case, I placed a yellow, legal-sized piece of paper with my own circle with the names of most everyone I could think of. Every time I'd play, I'd open that case, close my eyes and let my finger drop onto the paper. I would look at the names of the people I was touching, and play for them.

It's interesting that nearly half of the people I told of my decision to follow my dream – to become a professional musician and writer – remarked, "Wow! I wish I could do that!" I asked them, "Do you have kids in school?" (I thought if they did, it makes it much harder to start those big changes.) But many of them said, "No."

If they said no, I asked, "Then what's stopping you?" And I really meant it. Hey, grab the pen and write your script! That's precisely when I began pointing out to people, "It's Your Movie!"

The question now becomes: How would you *like* to influence your Circle of Influence? Some are young and impressionable. Some are older and impressionable. You have a great opportunity to impact them in a very positive way. Or, in the opposite way! *It's Your Movie!*

But like it or not, you *do* influence them. So, spark in them a light of kindness or compassion, or peace, or love. Touch all the people in your long shot with things you'd choose, as if they were paying attention.

They are!

From the director's chair:

How many people can you recall who have deeply influenced you?
How can you expand your Circle of Influence?
In what major ways have you impacted people?
Do you want your movie to influence the multitudes or to be a private screening?

The Close-Up

The most revealing shot of all, of course, is the close-up. A good close-up takes advantage of the scene's textures, shapes, and shading. It gives the audience a look at what otherwise would go unexamined.

In the context here – making your own movie – the close-up is of your life, and what you can discover about yourself upon closer examination. You'll find that you can move in for a close-up as frequently as you'd like, and reap the rewards on a regular basis.

Each time you do, you'll find genuine gratitude and appreciation for who you are, what you have, and what you can do. It's a heart-opening exercise.

You can also move in for a close-up in gratitude for all that you've received, from so many wonderful people.

On Thanksgiving, during the holiday season, and at birthdays, it's easy and appropriate to be grateful. And whenever you receive gifts, whether expected or not, it's normal courtesy to express thanks.

But why not today? Why not set aside time to remember all the extra-special gifts that have been presented to you over the years. Especially *your life!*

Without the Gift of Life, it would be really difficult to have been blessed with all the other gifts, true?

How do you view the Gift of Life? Do you believe life is a gift? Or is it a torture to be endured? Or neither. These are questions found "at the deep end of the pool." They get philosophical, spiritual, and can be analyzed ad infinitum.

When creating your most beautiful movie, can you envision life as a gift, a wonderful gift – an opportunity to be, to feel, to love and be loved? To make a difference? To recognize your natural talents and put them to use?

The opportunity to experience emotions, to learn the lessons, to grow and teach, to contribute, is such a gift!

Certainly, to think otherwise is understandable. You could look at the suffering of so many, at the devastation, hunger, poverty, abuse, and disease, and insist that life is no gift for millions. Who knows, or can even guess, why such sad elements exist on the same planet that provides such abundance and joy for others?

Could it be that it is the privilege of the affluent to help those in need? Could it be that it is *for* the affluent that those in need exist? Could it be that it is *for* those in need that the affluent exist? Maybe someday more will seriously help those in need, and less will ignore them. Maybe someday the disproportionate numbers will begin to shift so that more may view life as a gift.

As one of the blessed few, you can definitely choose to help, to share your abundance, to give time, talent, and treasure to those in need.

It is certainly something to work for and pray for. And when those prayers are answered, that will be something else to be thankful for. Maybe you could make that part of your movie.

Anybody reading this has been educated to a fairly exclusive degree, compared to the majority of the world's population. In fact, in the top 5% of the socio-economic scale. Imagine that! How blessed are you to have been born into that echelon!

Sure, life isn't sunshine and roses in every area, at every moment. But, given the luck of the draw, you did very well.

I have a wise friend who calls challenges in life, such as needing to repaint the den, or dealing with a bad hair day, "high-class problems." Not that she's tickled to have problems, but that when she puts things in perspective, she can lighten up a bit.

The long shot will give you an overview of your world, and the sweet connections that exist with others. Keeping those precious connections in mind, that's the time to move in for the close-up. And after every long shot and every close-up comes The Payoff.

From the director's chair:
What do you appreciate most about your personality? Possessions? Talents?
What new scenes can you write from a place of gratitude?
How does your gratitude affect others?

The Payoff

Every movie needs a payoff scene, just like every song needs a good, strong payoff line. It's the major hook that grabs the heart of the audience and seals the deal.

You have to plan the payoff scene in your movie very carefully. Let's take a moment and seriously think about it.

It could be peace, or joy, or love, or fame, or whatever you choose as your desired payoff. You get to pick the payoff. No judgment. No mistakes, or poor choices. Whatever you want to have, or to be.

When you're caught up in the "busy," that is, the seemingly urgent activities of everyday life, the days go by and you can get so consumed in doing that you forget you are, in fact, a human *being*.

Ever think of making a daily To Be list? I make mine before I start on my To Do list.

Take a moment every so often to detach from doingness, and look around, acknowledge whatever you're feeling, and direct your attention to *beingness*.

It's really not anything more than tuning into what you're feeling, and observing the experience.

The observation itself acts as a separator between yourself and the emotion, almost as though you're watching a big movie screen of your life, and you get to view you being you. Become aware of how you're responding to what's happening, and you can choose healthy ways to respond, and to exist.

Living this way, *intentionally*, lets you manage how you experience things moment by moment, and ultimately, how you experience life.

There is so much to be said for living in the moment, when you can know genuine joy. Yet, in the moment, you are not really conscious of the workings of things. You are truly in the *being*, completely engrossed in activity, to the extent that time flies, and you have no idea where it goes, because it's not even noticed.

When I'm writing, I'm so engaged that hours go by, and I can't tell you what time it is. Truly, when I'm writing, especially music, I feel more connected with God, more in line with my divine purpose, than at any other time, engaged in any other thing. I am in my bliss. But if I were asked if I felt joy, I would say I didn't really feel anything. I was busy being, not feeling.

Intentionally choose to let the worries of the future rest for the time being, and release, if only for a while, the regrets and resentments of the past. Just let them all float by themselves. Here's how it works:

Start off by getting comfortable and relaxing your body. Let your shoulders drop a little. Feel your heart beat more slowly. Inhale calm. Exhale tension. Concentrate on the air you're taking in, and sending out. Repeat that inhale and exhale process three times. Think of what or whom puts you in a true state of whatever your Payoff might be. You've been there before. So, recall one of those times. In your mind, you're back there again.

Recollect all the elements of the scene. Connect with that state, that Payoff, as much as possible. Become highly present to your connection to the divine. Feel extreme and genuine gratitude, and express it through the connection you experience.

A nice, healthy practice you can do whenever you'd like, and so much more fun than spending time in worry, regret or resentment.

When I realized that I got to pick my Payoff, I chose joy.

To me, joy is an interesting thing. It's not an emotion really, like happiness. It's more a state, such as Peace.

But pick your own payoff. And repeat those scenes often. Do it intentionally! I bet you'll enjoy the moments and discover a wonderful lesson or two.

From the director's chair:
How does your To Be list differ from your To Do list?
How can you make that Payoff scene clear and memorable?
What activity makes you feel most connected to the divine?
What would it take for you to create a plan for yourself that assures a Payoff daily? Why wait?

Let Out The Joy!

(Lyrics by Peter Schroeder)

There's something inside me that needs to break free.
It's been there a long, long time - an eternity.
It's close to the surface; it's bursting inside.
And now that the time is right, it won't be denied.

Let all the joy come out. Sing it out loud and clear.
It is what we're about. Let it begin right here.
Let Out The Joy!
Let Out The Joy!

There's something inside us, that we could all use,
To bring us together again. We've paid enough dues.
We all know the feeling. We share the desire.
When we all express our joy, we sound like a choir.

Let all the joy come out. Sing it out loud and clear.
It is what we're about. Let it begin right here.
Let Out The Joy!
Let Out The Joy!
Let Out The Joy!

'There's something inside you, now don't shake your head.
You know what I'm talking about. You've heard what I said.
And this is the moment for your Light to shine.
So, come, let us celebrate. Put your hand in mine!

Let all the joy come out. Sing it out loud and clear.
It is what we're about. Let it begin right here.
Let Out The Joy!
Let Out The Joy!
Let Out The Joy!
Let Out The Joy!

7

Closing Shots

The Lesson
The Message
The Happy Ending
Happy Trails

The Lesson

Every good film has a lesson or two that it sets out to impart to its audience. The same thing applies to this book. I've learned a whole bunch of lessons, most of which came as complete surprises.

The original title was *Intentional Living*. This is the philosophy at the heart of most everything I've written. And it is my strong intention that there will be a book out with that title, written by yours truly, some day.

The book people that I've dealt with thought *It's Your Movie!* had broader appeal, so the change was made.

I've had fun transforming these chapters into movie-themed messages.

Yes, the writing of this book has taught many lessons. And the one that I was brought back to time and again is the one I was intending to use for this very chapter – the boat is meant to be rowed *down* the stream.

I am referring to "Row, Row, Row Your Boat," of course. Its insight, its metaphysical, metaphorical brilliance, cannot be denied. The popular children's song describes merrily rowing one's boat down the stream, not up the stream. How profound is *that*? Did the lyricist enjoy boating? Did he and his friends have a rough day, rowing against the current? Did they even *have* a boat?

You and I will probably never know the answers, but regardless, the words fit nicely in making your own movie.

There is a flow to life. Once in a while, everything clicks, and you feel as if you're in the flow. It's a beautiful place to be.

And the flow is always there, moving in one direction. The river may bend, or widen, or narrow, but the current is always there, always available.

Creating a movie fits so well into the idea of a life-flow. You can set your intentions, and construct a plot, and if this conforms to the natural flow of life, the magic happens. The universe supports you in ways you could never imagine.

People (read: Angels) appear to assist you. Resources like money, time, shortcuts, and guides present themselves. It's as if your personal band of assistants, like a divine production team, shows up, out of nowhere, to carry you *down* that stream.

Sometimes, in your eagerness to get things done, or in your desire to stick to an agenda you are convinced is the only way, you encounter struggle and setbacks. The message here can be one of two:

Persevere; stay the course; stick to your convictions. Or...*you're swimming upstream. Hear what you're being told. Be flexible and find another path.*

So, how do you know which message to heed? The same way to approach any question: Let the answers come to you. Get your ego out of there. Be open and allow.

Inner Guides, your Higher Self, Intuition – the answers are known, and can be communicated to the conscious mind.

Set your intention to allow the answers to come. Then, let them.

Trust. There are bigger forces at work here than you know. That's precisely why intention has power. And that's why you can create your own movie.

That's why book titles get changed. And lessons can be learned with or without pain. Your job is to get in the boat. And row with the current.

The more you let it work for you, the more you trust it. The more you trust it, the more you are eager and willing for the current to take you, take you down, down, down the stream. Merrily. Intentionally.

From the director's chair:

What's the lesson you wish to impart from your movie?

How has the universe magically supported you in the past?

How do you know when you're swimming upstream? What can you do about it?

How can you be in the flow more often, letting the current take you?

The Message

Lessons are learned. Messages are delivered and received, and they come from all sorts of sources. What's the message you're receiving from this book?

I received a great message once from a greeting card. It said, "It only takes a moment to create a memory." And that's a message I'd like to communicate to you. Take a moment; make a memory.

The quote resonates as absolutely true to me. Like the picture that I have in my mind of my mother, waving from the window of her home; we all have so many memories.

We would be visiting my parents' home in the North Woods of Wisconsin, or we would be over on Sunday for dinner. As we'd leave, there she would be, in the window, waving. Simply a scene I'll never forget.

And there are countless scenes I can recall, with so many people from all over the world. Happy scenes, tender moments, colorful memories.

Our 13-year-old came home from school one day, announcing she had signed us up for a foreign exchange student. My wife was ecstatic. I was less than ecstatic – we need another teenager in the house?

Laure arrived from France knowing only a little English, and was quite shy. But in the hour it took to drive from the airport to our house, I told my wife that we would be going to her wedding some day. She was in our hearts that quickly.

We were able to visit her family the following year, and it was raining the day we left their home. As we pulled away, I could see Laure's face in the window, with a tear in her eye, waving. It's a moment I'll cherish always.

And France is now a favorite location to shoot scenes in my movie.

Every memory I have was created in a moment. My memories are actually snapshots of those moments. Usually, a strong emotion is attached to the memory. And it's safe to say that those moments were not *intentionally* made to be memorable.

So, let's relate that to creating your movie.

In any moment, you have the opportunity to create something special. This is easiest when a big event is about to take place. But imagine that you are experiencing memorable moments daily, really cherishing how beautiful a conversation, or a drive to the store, can be. Every day, if you're open to the possibility, is so full of moments that could be held as extraordinary.

Elevate your level of awareness to what's taking place at any given moment. Look around right now. Is there beauty to behold in the surroundings? Is there an energy to be felt, a pulse or rhythm of everything going on at this instant?

Further, be highly mindful of the way you choose to observe, and the way you choose to respond, and the meaning that you give things. Each decision you make about reacting to what goes on out there is what makes all the difference in the quality of your life.

You make that sunset beautiful or sad, or that fire in the fireplace romantic or depressing, or that dinner memorable or forgettable, or that rough argument useful or hurtful, or that flat tire a great lesson or a nuisance.

Of themselves, moments are just points in time. They have absolutely no meaning until you give them meaning. This is one of the divine gifts that you have been given – the ability to be conscious of or ignore, appreciate or denigrate, be grateful or resentful – for anything you want, anytime, anywhere. You choose.

In fact, look for moments to remember every day. If you look for them, you'll find some. But if you never look, how are you going to find any?

And as you open your heart to add your love, or compassion, or exuberance to a moment, it can indeed become a memory. Why not make a memory now? Make it a highlight of your movie! Every moment, every day can have its own beautiful memory, and these memories can form a series of Happy Endings.

From the director's chair:
What messages have you received from this book?
What are your strongest, most beautiful images of the past?
How many different meanings can you give to a recent scene?
If you were going to make a memory now, what would it be?

The Happy Ending

In the Big Movie, otherwise referred to as the Big Picture, when do we get to see the happy ending? It seems as though there is no happy ending in sight. In fact, it seems to become more remote by the minute.

There are tragedies in life that are painful and sad. There are mystifying and incomprehensible events that defy all attempts at rational explanation.

Life happens. However, there is, even in the most devastating situation, an opportunity for good (or improvement) to result from it. I know it is often clouded by unfair losses, hardships, pain, etc., but consider the possibility.

War is horrible. The Holocaust was despicable. Child and spousal abuse. Disease. Poverty. Hunger. Mental and emotional illness. The list is long. The list is sobering. So confounding – what's the cause? So frustrating – what can be done?

Time is a great resource for regaining some semblance of strength to carry on. In time, there is always some useful residue that is a consequence of a tragedy. The value may be miniscule compared to the pain, but the pain may spawn a passion to positively affect the future.

When you're creating your movie, use the Big Picture for support; shift your focus from the pain and anger to the understanding that there are things unknown. And remember that the effects of our actions may lead to places that can't be anticipated.

What if, ultimately, every chosen path leads to good? It's a choice, an option. Make the one that serves you best, for right now. Down the road, you can and may change our mind.

If you subscribe to the Theory of Order and deliberately opt for a goodness to things, then you can know hope, and perhaps comfort. In Nature, there are events commonly called tragic, such as earthquakes, hurricanes, floods, droughts, etc. They are part of the balance, the ecosystem. And from tragedies come what is commonly known as "good."

There are heroes and rescuers; there are workers providing aid and comfort and relief who are fulfilling their life's purpose. For the survivors, there can be a profound sense of perspective about what is important. And there is constant regeneration of the Earth.

This does not discount or minimize the pain.

The beauty of Nature endures. Love persists. Good exists. And whatever happens, *whatever happens*, it means what *you* decide it means. Nothing more.

The happy ending starts when you say it starts. Who is to say it hasn't already started? Or it started long ago? Or it's always been happy? Or it's never going to be happy?

You choose happy. Or you choose sad. You choose whichever you want. And you can change our mind whenever you want.

It's totally and completely up to you.

For me, I'd prefer to live with hope, with optimism – which some might call idiotic, or pollyannic. (There's a new word, Mr. Webster!) But it's my choice. I'd rather feel happy. I'd rather be smiling, grateful, feeling connected to God. And I get to choose because it's my movie.

As a child, I used to sit under the dining room table with my cousin, Linda, by my side. The lace tablecloth would be hanging over the edge, but we could see the tiny, black and white TV screen. We'd watch The Roy Rogers Show. Roy and Dale would always win.

And the happy ending would always end with that song Linda and I would sing with Roy and Dale.

So, here it is:

Happy trails to you, until we meet again.
Happy trails to you, keep smiling until then.
Who cares about the clouds when we're together?
Just sing a song and bring the sunny weather.
Happy trails to you, till we meet again.
(Lyrics by Dale Evans)

Happy trails to you as you create a great movie for yourself!

Epilogue – It's A Wrap!

Creating a place to visit, revisit, and breathe easy, with perhaps some stimulation or inspiration, a place to examine or re-examine your attitudes, priorities, opinions, responses, habits, teachings. That has been my objective while creating this work, *It's Your Movie!*

I think of it as a retreat from the action and urgency of the day. You have so many chances to fill the next moments with the pressing tasks at hand that you could, undoubtedly, fill your days, and thus your life with nothing but tackling the most urgent issues – the ones that seem to have the loudest voices. And more often than not, they are the issues of other good folk.

So, how do you find the time to reflect purely and solely on you? I feel these would be moments of high importance, to deal with both your urgent and long-term matters with care.

If you don't consciously make sure the time is set aside for it, magic will not make it happen. It is strictly your choice.

Hopefully, *It's Your Movie!* has planted some seeds, presented some new provocations, and piqued your curiosity. Hopefully, you will allow what resonates within you to initiate a shift within you, and express yourself a bit differently, maybe even radically. And hopefully, others will notice what you're doing and saying, the new choices you're making, and they'll become inspired.

Ripples expand. Breezes will blow.
Changes will come, someday, I know
    from *Imagine the Difference* by the author.

Be the change you'd like to see.
Act the way you'd like others to be.
    from *To Change the World* by the author.

There is a beautiful concept introduced by author Neale Donald Walsch called "The First Domino" that acknowledges the fact that every product, organization, change, etc., begins with one person taking a thought and going with it. One person, who has a contagious enthusiasm that affects colleagues, supporters, and even successors. That person is called The First Domino, from which all processes are set in motion.

There is another concept I love called "Critical Mass." This term is defined as "the smallest mass of fissionable material that will support a self-sustaining chain reaction." A self-sustaining chain reaction! If enough individuals share a dream or an attitude, a critical mass will be reached and the chain reaction can begin. And it will be self-sustaining!

So, those are the two ingredients that I see blended together into this delicious vision:

We may never be a First Domino,
but any one of us could be a Critical Mass-maker!

You or I could be the straw that breaks the old way of

coexistence that slogs along in war, and hate, and violence, and abuse, and sad ignorance. And that is why we have got to do whatever comes to us to promote and express and *live* the way we want things to be for our selves and our children and our grandchildren and our world, for all future generations.

Discover what is most important to you in this world; learn whatever you are naturally good at. Then, pursue a life that lets you express whatever is most important to you. Don't be afraid – you're helping the world! And use your most natural talents in some way – as a career or a volunteer or a part-time enthusiast.

All this is part of *It's Your Movie!,* and at the core of Intentional Living. All this is available to you. All you have to do is choose it, and let go of the old stuff.

Are you ready? Start creating your movie right now! With intention!

Appendix

Questions and Answers on Intentional Living

As mentioned in the chapter "The Lesson," Intentional Living is the philosophy that was the original inspiration for this book. The following questions and answers are meant to put this philosophy into practical applications.

INTENTIONAL LIVING DEFINED

Q. What exactly do you mean by Intentional Living? I'd like a specific definition.

A. I have an intention in mind, and I act and think in line with that intention. If I intend to raise as much as I can for my favorite charity, or, conversely, if I intend to embezzle as much as I can from my workplace, everything I think and do supports that intention. This book, this space of written words expressing my contentions, focuses on creating intentions that benefit (in my opinion) the individual as well as the world. Intents such as peace, kindness, joy, love, compassion, and honesty are ideas suggested here, because they are my intentions for living. What are yours?

THINGS CHANGE IN TIME

Q. Is Intentional Living for everyone? I have a friend who says it's bogus.

A. Your friend is entitled to his or her opinion. If it doesn't register with them, it's not for them right now. It may never be for them, and things change in time. As a child, I didn't like the taste of some vegetables, but I do now. In time, your friend may start asking different questions of himself. There may come a time when he begins to search for answers to these new questions. I bet you'll ask new questions as you grow. And I'll do it, too. Some are fortunate to hear those new questions at an early age. And some are fortunate to hear new questions in their later years. Whenever it happens, it's perfect.

TIME WELL-SPENT

Q. Every morning, I plan my day. I have a to-do list that usually keeps me busy all day. How can I fit intentions in? I barely have time to read the paper.

A. Intentional Living is really not an exhausting, time-consuming endeavor. It's basically a mental exercise that you do periodically. It's like fixing a leaky roof. It requires some time and effort, but the effects last a long time, and actually, learning about yourself is fun! I'd suggest you make an entry on your to-do list: "Discover what's really important to me." What *is* important to you? What principles and convictions resonate most deeply? If you were going to describe the *you* who you'd most like to be, what character traits would you include? Believe me, this is time well-spent. You'll learn great things about yourself, and you can gain lots of time in the process by dropping things that don't support your true intentions. Then relax, and, maybe, read the paper!

FORGETTING "SHOULD"

Q. With the speed of life being faster than ever, I feel it's important to slow down regularly and smell the Starbucks. Shouldn't balance be everyone's intention? Aren't there some basic, common intentions for everybody?

A. There's that word "should." It's a delicate matter, but I don't think one should use "should." I've got a friend who calls a *should* an ego-rule. Everyone has ego-rules, and they create messes like "mine are better than yours." I think balance in life is a good thing, but to try to assemble a group of intentions, ones that "should" be on all lists, seems useless. Balance may be important to you, but there are focused, well-intentioned people who have no desire to have balance in their lives. And I can understand this. And they might have some intentions that you or I would never have. And that's cool.

ABOUT GOOD INTENTIONS

Q. People have intentions all the time. My mother says, "The road to hell is paved with good intentions." Intentions are good only if you carry them out.

A. Ah, the old "road to hell" argument. Intentions, even the best of intentions, are hollow without the substance of follow-through. Intentional Living always speaks of two parts. The first part is discovering what's most important to you, what resonates most strongly in you. That's the intention part. Once you've identified those principles and convictions, you let them guide you in life. Demonstrate daily that you are principled. Walk your talk, as they say. That's the second part, the "Living" part. The road to hell may be paved with good intentions, as mothers all over the world declare. But the road to peace is paved with good intentions lived. Pass it on; tell that to *your* kids.

FORGETTING SHOULD – PART II

Q. I've always had a problem figuring out what's most important in life. Or really, what should be most important in life. How does one know for sure?

A. There are a few different ways to go with your question: the *"should"* issue, the "for sure" issue, and the most/least important issue. The closest you'll come to "for sure" is to seek the answers within. Close your eyes. Breathe slowly and deeply. Ask yourself your questions. *Let* the answers come to you. Don't edit with judgment. Honor whatever you receive. Some call this meditation. That's your best source for what's true for you. "Should" implies other people – parents, society, etc. Again, go inside and you will get *your* answers. Forget "should." Finally, the *most* important will show up when you meditate. Trust the process – your Inner Wisdom knows. And know that your answers will surely evolve in time.

ABOUT LABELS

Q. This past election has been so bad for our country because of the division it has caused, and there are such strong negative opinions about "the other side." What can be done to get everyone back together?

A. Understand the meanings you give things. "Bad" or "good" (two popular assessments of the election) shows how any one thing is just a thing, with no meaning, until it is tagged with a label by someone. The results were the results. They can be construed as many things. Remember what is most important to you. Live by your principles. Collectively, we choose our future. How do you respond to things you label *bad*? With anger? Vengeance? Compassion? Fear? Curiosity? Hope? If you want everyone back together, what will you choose?

STICK WITH IT

Q. I like starting things, like new health programs. But I always slide off them after a while, even though that's not my intention. Any suggestions?

A. Everyone has intentions, and lives in accordance with these intentions. Always. It's common for some to start things, like diets or exercise programs, and then regularly slide off, as you say. It's because of two things acting at the same time: the motivation that was strong at the start begins to wane, and a hidden saboteur begins to talk more loudly. The way to stick with something is to make effective reminders of your original motivation. (If it was powerful enough on day one, it can work on day twenty-one.) Recognize that voice of your internal saboteur, and tell it that you're on to it and you're not going to cooperate any more. Keep the vision clear and bright in your mind, and be stronger than the distractions.

LET'S BE PRACTICAL

Q. I wonder: how possible is Intentional Living in the real world? It seems like it's a good theory, but not very practical.

A. Let's talk about the practical side of it. Personally, it strikes me as exceedingly practical because it offers a focused approach to life. With no intention, much time and energy is expended on worry (fearing the future) and/or regret and resentment (sadness and bitterness over the past). Intentional Living deals with decisions at hand, as current moments on a single path. With no intention, time and energy is spent on following the instructions and teachings of others. But Intentional Living encourages each individual to find their own True North. I say, "Be practical – save time and energy – live with intention."

INTENTIONS AND WEIGHT LOSS

Q. I've been trying to lose weight for years. Can Intentional Living help?

A. If you are serious about losing weight, you should consult a specialist. Find one who comes with terrific references. Then I would follow the advice and instructions of the specialist from an Intentional Living perspective. Make their program part of your daily intention. Make it a high priority because you understand and believe the benefits that would be available to you as you lose weight. Good health can and should be a life-long intention. It's a natural way to honor yourself. The healthier you are, the more you can contribute to the world, and the more you can be a great example to those around you.

HEALTHFUL INTENTIONS

Q. I have a few health issues. I have money challenges. I have little or no fun. Where do I start? I have one big intention to change everything.

A. It can seem overwhelming at times, and exhausting just thinking about everything. But, there is hope. And, there are answers. Find a quiet spot. Go inside. Breathe deeply, slowly, and let yourself sink. Breathe in calm; breathe out tension. Ask for guidance. Sink deeper. Allow whatever you experience to happen without your own judgment, or resistance. Stay out of your ego. Don't think; just let the guidance come. Each solution starts with a first step. This is your first step. It will lead you to your second step, and on from there. There is an order which you will discover is best for you. Follow the order that you feel as you receive guidance. Accept. It can all be done. You and your staff of assistants (that is, the Universe) can do it.

INTENTIONS AND PEOPLE

Q. I like this concept of Intentional Living – I find it appealing. But we all live in a world with other people, and other people always get in the way.

A. Do other people get in the way? Let's say you've set your intentions. Now, people/opportunities come your way. This is what the Universe brings you. And what do you do with what the Universe brings you? You use it. You learn the lessons being offered. You are thankful for the teachers who appear, and you pay attention. And you learn. People really don't get in the way. People *lead* the way! However, you may have the intention to prove that you're a hopeless victim. Very common. But are you ready to shed the victim's clothing? Are you ready to be a student? Are you ready to be a teacher? Be true to your intentions and watch others pay attention to you.

GLOBAL INTENTIONS

Q. I know that Intentional Living thinks that life is absolutely fair. Why, then, the child abuse, and senseless violence? No one can say that is fair.

A. Sometimes, it's not easy to face the truth, but there are causes for everything. We, as a human race, bring on everything that is happening today in our world – the good (that which produces pleasure) and the bad (that which produces pain). The outer world reflects our inner world. There is a collective unconscious that is governed by natural law. Be how you want the world to be. As more people give up hate, violence, etc., the critical mass will be reached and the world will shift, and seem less unfair. Choose your world. *Cause* your world.

THE START OF FORGIVENESS

Q. These times seem to be fraught with animosity. More than ever, people are intolerant, angry, and hateful toward those with different opinions, lifestyles, and values. I can't stand them! Why can't people just get along?

A. Your feelings are shared by many. And for every problem, there is a solution. Some very wise minds have suggested, "Be the change you want to see." That is, act the way you'd like others to act. Think the way you'd like others to think. If you'd like others to "get along" and be tolerant, become tolerant of those who now get under your skin. It starts by trying to understand the opinions and feelings of others. As you begin to understand their motivation, you can begin to convert your blame and confusion into curiosity and compassion. This is the start of forgiveness. Once you forgive, the separation disappears and the connection can be established.

BE HONEST WITH YOURSELF

Q. Every morning, I plan, and every night, I review, but it seems like nothing really changes, even though I try Living Intentionally. What am I doing wrong?

A. Wrong is an interesting word to use here. What could you be doing wrong? If nothing seems to have changed, perhaps that's how you want it to be. If you contend that you'd like some different results, either do things differently, or investigate what you really want. Hint: look around – it's what you really want. Just because you might verbalize a desire for a different life, you might actually want to keep from changing. You may find safety or justice in staying as you are. Look inside. Be honest with yourself. If you really want to change, start changing.

THE REASON FOR EVERYTHING

Q. I would like to believe there is a reason for everything, but some wars, and crimes, and horrible things don't make sense. What's that all about?

A. It is a common belief that everything happens for a reason, that there are causes and effects that are part of our experience as we know it. We are currently a global society focusing and dealing with symptoms, not causes. We don't attempt to confront or discuss the causes of war, or crimes, or "horrible" things, and so they continue to pervade our planet. Eventually, I believe, we will realize our need to attend to causes, and we'll probably do that the day we realize that it's the most economical approach. There *is* a reason for everything. The reason is us.

INTENTION WORKS

Q. How does Intentional Living and money work? I've set an intention to have more money, and it doesn't happen.

A. First of all, intention works. Setting an intention is the first step. Next, be open to the opportunities that come your way. Follow what the universe brings you. If you do this, your intention can't help but be fulfilled. Unless. (This is the courageous, honest, gotta-face-it part.) Unless you have a conflicting belief or intention that you hold more strongly than, let's say, accumulating a sum of money. That belief could be that you're undeserving, or you may have the intention to prove that you're a hopeless victim. These are both very common situations. But uncover that deep, debilitating belief or intention, and understand it for what it was – useful to get you to where you are now.

FINDING THE GIFTS

Q. I've heard it said that everyone is in their perfect place. How can this be if I'm not feeling well, or have some disease?

A. Sometimes, it's not easy to find the perfection of our situation. If illness or disease is what you're experiencing at a particular time, you might wonder, "How can this be perfect?" In the big picture, however, there is a gift in everything. Even things that are painful contain gifts. You may not discover or comprehend the gifts instantly, but when you shift your perspective, you can find them. Illness may force you to slow down and contemplate your life, and make some changes. You may be better able to relate to others' illness. You can learn to receive care from others that you might otherwise find difficult to accept. There are always, always, lots of gifts when you look from the heart.

A PLACE OF AWARENESS

Q. I want to be open and spontaneous. If I'm always living intention-

ally, how can I be open to new things, or available to what the Universe presents to me?

A. Intentional Living is about being. It never precludes being open and spontaneous. Anything you may encounter throughout the day can be dealt with based upon your intention for living. If someone calls with tickets to a play for the evening, you can choose to go or not based on how either choice would line up with your intention for the evening. Not that you necessarily are going to have an intention for every hour of your life, but you can certainly consider your highest intentions when deciding anything. *If you choose.* Just come from a place of awareness, as opposed to ignorance.

CHOOSING INTENTIONALLY

Q. I can only inject my intentions occasionally in my life, and only in certain areas (not work or romance), because others are in control. So, why bother?

A. Your boss may "control" what you *do* at work, but you are always the one who applies meaning to everything you do, say, and think, and to how you respond to what happens around you. You can always thoughtfully weigh the consequences of your options, and choose intentionally, so your choice conforms with your values and priorities. Others are in control only when you allow them to be. Perhaps you've been trained from early on to give control (power) to others.

Romance, for example, can be a level, interdependent relationship, or tilted, where one has a majority of the influence, decision-making, and power/control. Ultimately, of course, you choose your place.

PRACTICING AWARENESS

Q. Some people say it's good to live in the moment, while others say you have to plan for the future. How does Intentional Living deal with this paradox?

A. First of all, it's not a paradox. One can be planning for the future, while being in the moment. And one can be in the moment while planning for the future. Same thing. "In the moment," "living in the now," "staying in the present" all mean to be mindful, or conscious of where one is, and of what one is doing at that moment. While you're preparing a trip, or remembering an event, you can be aware that "Here I am, preparing for a trip," or "Here I am, remembering an event." Being aware – that's the key here. You're reading this now, absorbing, thinking, maybe judging, while you're breathing, and your heart is pumping, and so many other things are going on. Intentional Living emphasizes practicing awareness of our thoughts, feelings, and actions.

IT'S ALWAYS YOUR CHOICE

Q. Over the years, I have grown skeptical and cynical. How can anyone not be?

A. To be sure, there are reasons one can find every day to justify skepticism and cynicism. I would simply encourage you to not throw out the baby with the bath water. There are many, many wonderful reasons to be open and trusting and loving, without being naïve or gullible. Your cynicism/skepticism is your choice. Keep that attitude and you will undoubtedly encounter numerous situations that will help you prove you are right to feel that way. That's part of Intentional Living. You'll find whatever you believe is out there. Ask yourself, what is my attitude costing me? Joy? Peace of mind? There are millions of folks who enjoy life in the very world in which you live. So, you get to choose.

End Credits

I have been blessed with a glorious cast of support. First, last and always is Anne, who encourages me and loves me like no other. James let his light shine with illustrations. Marv and Liberty Lincoln, of Thunder Mountain Productions, dove in with me, and guided me to safety. Peggy graced me with her art. Anugito's artistic hand is found throughout this book. My CSC chums, Mike, Dave, Tom, and Terry, gave me the feedback that made the difference. John made recording more enjoyable and sound better than ever. And finally, Anne lights my way, pushes me, demands integrity and high standards, and talks and listens. What don't we share?

Thanks, in advance, to the publishing company that shares my vision for this work, and signs me to an exclusive contract. Your wisdom is matched by few. Your taste is not to be underestimated. Your trust shall be rewarded many times over.

Peter Schroeder

Peter is an author, singer-songwriter, and seminar leader. He has developed and conducted personal growth workshops, including Intentional Health, Priorities, Priorities For Partners, and Find Your Dream/Live Your Dream. Peter has written and performed over 100 songs in his genre Intentional Music. His songs commonly form the bases for the chapters of It's Your Movie!

Born in the Chicago suburbs, Peter moved to Nashville to pursue his music career. There he recorded much of his body of material, and performed in clubs – singing both his own material and covering songs from artists as diverse as Elvis, Ray Charles and Jimmy Buffett. In 2004, he and his wife fulfilled a long-time dream and moved to Sedona, Arizona, where he continues to lead workshops and counsel couples and individuals on career and life issues.

Contact Peter by e-mail at pete@peteschroeder.com.

About the CD

The free CD attached to this book is a sampler of the songs on Peter Schroeder's first CD, titled *Let Out the Joy*. This release, which contains 12 original songs, is available online at www.peteschroeder.com. Many of the song lyrics in this book (which serve as the soundtrack for *It's Your Movie!*), are also on the CD.

Contact Peter by e-mail at pete@peteschroeder.com.